Get in Rob, get in

Ali ran and ran to get help.

"Dad, Dad, Rob fell.
Rob fell down."

Rob's dad and
Ali's dad can help.

Rob's dad ran.

Ali's dad ran.

Ali's dad helps Rob's dad.
Ali helps.
Ali gets a big net.

Down went Rob's dad.
Down he went.

Up went Rob and
up went Rob's dad.

Rob and Spot and Ali